POET'S ENGLAND 14

SHROPSHIRE

Compiled by Neil Griffiths and John Waddington-Feather

Illustrated by Gillian Durrant

GW00384251

Brentham Press

First published 1994 by
Brentham Press, 40 Oswald Road, St Albans, Herts AL1 3AQ

ISBN   0 905 772 39 3

British Library Cataloguing-in-Publication Data.
A catalogue record for this book is available from the British Library.

DTP by Gillian Durrant
Printed in England by Antony Rowe Ltd, Chippenham, Wilts SN14 6QA

FOREWORD

One of Britain's most beautiful though lesser-known counties, Shropshire borders on eight others, three of them Welsh. For centuries in the Middle Ages it housed garrisons protecting the Welsh Marcher lands, until Wales came under the sovereignty of the Plantagenets and England under the rule of the Tudors. Many Shropshire towns had alternative Welsh names, including its capital, Shrewsbury, which was known as Pengwern. Even today, on market days, Welsh is heard as frequently as English in Shrewsbury and Oswestry.

The county is split almost equally in two by the River Severn, and the Severn Gorge at Ironbridge is generally recognised as the birthplace of the Industrial Revolution in the 18th century. The whole area now locates the biggest open-air museum in Europe over the early industrial sites. To the north the county flattens out to the Cheshire plain; to the south is the hill country which stretches to Herefordshire.

Much of Shropshire's beauty lies in the very varied geology and building styles. The limestone of Wenlock Edge produces the grey stone walls and cottages of the east. Elsewhere the red sandstone and greystones have left their mark on the landscape and buildings. More distinctive features are the black and white houses which abound in its towns and villages. Shrewsbury and Ludlow have superb examples in their inns and huge medieval merchants' town mansions.

Shropshire has a long literary tradition, though never a prolific one. To date, few great writers have come out of Shropshire, probably because its population has been so sparse and rural; possibly because its chief industry for many years has been agriculture. Farmers are happier manipulating ploughs than pens! But that does not necessarily mean they are not poetic.

Shropshire produced one famous Elizabethan poet, Sir Philip Sidney, and a twentieth-century woman novelist/poet, Mary Webb. John Milton set his masque 'Comus' in the Shropshire countryside and it was first produced at Ludlow Castle, the setting still for annual productions of English classical drama. The war-poet, Wilfred Owen, was born at Oswestry and lived in Shrewsbury for much of his life. A.E. Housman, a Worcestershire man, adopted the county and his collection of poems 'A Shropshire Lad' bear testimony to his love of the region. However, for much of our anthology we have relied on contemporary poets, which is a pleasing feature, because their inclusion reflects the growing 'colonies' of writers and artists in several parts of the county; also its increasingly cosmopolitan character.

1994   *Neil Griffiths and John Waddington-Feather*

ACKNOWLEDGMENTS

We are indebted to the following for their helpful co-operation in the provision of historical information for this anthology: Elizabeth Anderton, Rev. Tom Boulcott, Keith Griffiths, Michael Holmes, Guy Stapleton and the staff of the Wem branch of Shropshire County Libraries.

For permission to reproduce copyright material acknowledgement is made to: John Murray (Publishers) Ltd for 'A Shropshire Lad' by John Betjeman from Old Lights for New Chancels (1940). The Society of Authors, representing the estate of John Masefield, for 'The Shropshire Friends' from *In Glad Thanksgiving* (Heinemann, 1966).

Special thanks are due to a number of mainly local contributors who have provided both previously published and new material for the anthology. Unless otherwise acknowledged, copyright is held by the authors.

Poems are dated by their first year of publication where this is known.

SHROPSHIRE: Map showing
main places mentioned in the text

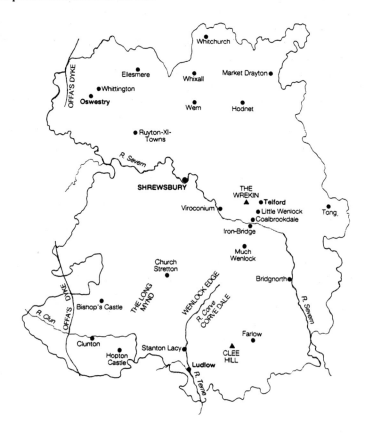

CONTENTS

I am of Shropshire, my shinnes be sharpe:
Ley wode to the fyre and dresse me my harpe.

16th C   *John Leland*

from
POLYOLBION

To Salop when her selfe cleere Sabrine comes to showe,
And wisely her bethinks the way shee had to goe,
South-west-ward casts her course; & with an amorous eye
Those Countries whence shee came, survayeth (passing by)
Those Lands in Ancient times old Cambria claym'd her due,
For refuge when to her th'oppressed Britans flew.;
By England now usurp't, who (past the wonted Meeres,
Her sure and soveraigne banks) had taken sundry Sheeres,
Which shee her Marches made: whereby those Hills of fame
And Rivers stood distrac't; accounting it their shame,
That all without that Mound which Mercian Offa cast
To runne from North to South, athwart the Cambrian wast,
Could England not suffice, but that the Straggling Wye,
Which in the hart of Wales was some-time said to lye,
Now onely for her bound proud England did prefer...

1622   *Michael Drayton*

from
THE SCHOOLMISTRESS

Admired Salopia! that with venial pride
Eyes her bright form in Severn's ambient wave,
Famed for her loyal cares in perils try'd,
Her daughters lovely, and her striplings brave.

1742   *William Shenstone*

from
THE SHROPSHIRE MILITIA

Since the Shropshire Militia is now to be rais'd,
The Shropshire Militia by me shall be prais'd.
While others but trot, my muse rides full gallop,
To sing to some tune the Militia of Salop.

The great Earl of Bath, the county's lieutenant,
Has gathered together the very best men on't,
All ready with swords in their hands to advance,
'Gainst Popish invasion, from Spain or from France.

Lord Pulteney the colonel, so bold and so brave,
To Portugal's gone, his country to save,
Like a lion he fought at Valentia they say,
For true glory all, without profit or pay.

The lieutenant colonel, the great squire Lawley,
In courage as great as a Haske or a Hawley,
From Staffordshire comes, with pleasure we hear,
To head the militia of merry Shropshire.

The lieutenants and ensigns to name in my song
Most folks will allow would make it too long;
In short, they are all such brave gentlemen,
That the like in all England you'll not meet again.

I think in my heart 'twould beat Shrewsbury Show,
To see these brave officers all in a row;
When so gallant a sight upon the parade is,
Take care of your hearts, ye fair Shropshire ladies.

But my bold country lads, let none fear to go,
With such noble commanders, to face the proud foe;
Who boldly will venture their fortunes and lives,
To fight for your property, sweet-hearts and wives.

Then join in the regiment, all lads of true spirit,
Where preferment will always tend upon merit,
And by act of parliament, as you well know,
There's no-one can force you from England to go.

And now, of my ballad pray don't make a jest,
To honour the county, I have done my best;
Then fill up a glass of Joe Laurence's beer,
And drink to the lads of merry Shropshire.

1762   *Anon*

from
A SHROPSHIRE LAD (XL)

Into my heart an air that kills
  From yon far country blows:
What are those blue remembered hills,
  What spires, what farms are those?

That is the land of lost content,
  I see it shining plain,
The happy highways where I went
  And cannot come again.

1896   *A.E. Housman*

THE SHROPSHIRE HILLS

In Shropshire, where the orange sky
Frames the purple hills,
I feel the strength of centuries
Rejuvenate my soul.

I roamed here with a kindred spirit once.
Together we were going to build a world
Where harmony and human kindness reigned.

Ambition intervened.
We joined the race for loot,
Accepted status quo.
But sometimes, when I see the Shropshire hills,
I live again the dreams of long ago.

1994   *Phyllis Fountain*

SHROPSHIRE

Time was
When ice sheets
Covered the Shropshire Plain
And all was void.

Time was
When melt-ice flowed
And rivers ran
And Severn then
Began its long and tortuous
Journey from the hills
Gouging its way through rocks
And earth in search
Of open sea.

Time was
When Romans marched
And built their roads
And founded settlements
As Uriconium – now Wroxeter.

Time was
When bloody battles raged
And arrows flew
And ragged soldiers
Died on Shropshire soil,
When kings and queens and princes
Passed along the dusty miles
And paused before the gates
Of Shrewsbury.

Time was
When men dug deep
For lead
For coal
When iron was smelted
In a quiet gorge
To build a bridge.

Time was
When railways came
To scar the land
And break apart the fields
And brooding hills.

Time is
When ribbon motorways
Extend their tentacles
To gobble up more land
For man to ride more speedily
In petrol-driven tins.

Time was –
Time is –
What will
In time to be?

1994   *Margaret Colledge*

from
A SHROPSHIRE LAD (L)

Clunton and Clunbury,
Clungunford and Clun,
Are the quietest places
Under the sun.

In valleys of springs of rivers,
  By Ony and Teme and Clun,
The country for easy livers,
  The quietest under the sun.

We still had sorrows to lighten,
  One could not be always glad,
And lads knew trouble at Knighton
  When I was a Knighton lad.

By bridges that Thames runs under,
  In London, the town built ill,
'Tis sure small matter for wonder
  If sorrow is with one still.

And if as a lad grows older
  The troubles he bears are more,
He carries his griefs on a shoulder
  That handselled them long before.

Where shall one halt to deliver
  This luggage I'd lief set down?
Not Thames, not Teme is the river,
  Nor London nor Knighton the town:

'Tis a long way further than Knighton,
  A quieter place than Clun,
Where doomsday may thunder and lighten
  And little 'twill matter to one.

1896   *A E Housman*

THE SHADE
(for Rosamund Andrew)

In God's quiet Shropshire acre
I southward look and see
The long slow line of Wrekin
Blue mist-hazed distantly.

And think me straight of Housman,
That lyrist sad in song,
His irony, his pity
For all the cosmic wrong.

Today the wood's untroubled
Along by Wenlock's side,
And April's sung in birdsong
This sundanced Eastertide.

Though still the shade of Housman
Goes glooming darkly wise,
For whom delight was blighted,
For whom Christ did not rise.

1994   *Frederic Vanson*

THE SHROPSHIRE FRIENDS

Long since, when coming from the West,
With England near, I could not rest,
Though night time fell,
So near the two that I loved best.

There, somewhere, nor-nor-east from me,
Was Shropshire, where I longed to be,
Ercall and Mynd,
Severn and Wrekin, you and me.

So up I went, to walk the deck,
To gaze, with eager aching neck,
For England's Lights,
The Lighthouses preventing wrecks.

Far forward I would crane, to spy
Those fixed stars of the sailor's eye,
His most loved stars,
And feel their beauty drawing nigh.

There, while the beating engines shed
The mumble of their trampled tread,
The ship's great heart,
I stared into the night ahead.

Into a darkness now I stare
Towards where Wrekin lifts in air
And Severn glides,
I know that you are somewhere there.

1966   *John Masefield*

THE DREAMING HILLS

Bring him, bud, changeling
– but a fine roseface – to this road,
midsummery, piping

with goldcrest, and even now, wind-fresh:
– stand him here, the lamb,
young frisker, monkey,
the sorrowful clay, – here,
by the low fence: make him stare –

there – at the blue-
green pillows, the patchworked
moveless billows, rounding and rounding

away, clefted darkly
with tree-violet and navy.

Will he still? – can peace-drip
invade his uncomprehended material? –
a bruisedness born, he could have done
with past-poured holy water: –

cries to fly –
he would not be surprised – runs,
leaping and flapping,
alongside the hills'
old bluey dreaming, old old sleeping.

1994   *V. Carlin*

INCOMERS
(to Shropshire)

We arrived with bags, baggage
and dreams, on a February
day when winter's
grip was gloved in iron;
yet there were lambs
in the fields at our gate.

Three hard years have shambled
through the seasons as we
struggle, still, to restore
a much neglected house to fit
the scheme of things
that brought us to this shire.

Disappointment has been the salt
in our daily bread, then
comes a bee-stung summer morning
with honey on its breath;
the foxy autumn nights
beneath a razzle-dazzle moon

and, always on the very edge
of winter's grim estate, lambs
promising spring
in the fields at our gate.

1994   *Brenda Whincup*

AUTUMN FIELD

Beneath this patient autumn field
History lies smouldering;
Above it faint miasmas rise,
Wafts of fire and melting rock and flood.
The bones of men, their livelihood;
Their barns, their crops, their homes,
Crumbled all to dust now yield
This russet-glowing ploughed earth.
With purple shadows flickering
In undulating furrows fold on fold,
It breathes of stirring life.

Hovering over some a film of green;
Others in quick growth glow emerald
Through the rust-brown mould.

Gilded by the burnished sun
At its low westering,
Drifts of brown and gold
Brim the ditches and the dwarfed hedgerow...
The trees have shed their wealth of summer green.

We draw long draughts of autumn air,
Breathe in the future and the long-ago.
Time stands still in this magic, bright-brief season,
And all of time is here.

1992   *Margery Lea*

16

VISIONS OF SUMMER

The gorse is in full bloom 'round Oakengates,
And saffron crocuses have dared to show their heads;
In Ercall Woods the nesting birds proclaim
An early Spring. We gather hopefully these threads
Which hint that Winter's failed, and fingers crossed, we wait
For lazy Summer days, and Shropshire lanes
Filled with the scent of honeysuckle and the sound
Of bees. We dream of hours spent wandering
Among the Stretton Hills, of sleeping villages
Quiet in the sun, of streams meandering
Through lush fields filled with ripening corn and all around
The song of larks. The mind envisages
Warm days, endless, under a cloudless sky.
Meanwhile the Wrekin waits – and so do I.

1989   *Allister Fraser*

OFFA'S DYKE

A stile to the past and you're on it,
minding your plodding, watching
your steps in the fern, rough-trekking
through the ruts and occasional cowpat
under the trees; hot and brooding,
tugged by the hills and the sun.

Offa's Dyke, it strides on
over the uplands. It crosses
hollows, forests and farms
on its Marches. Does Offa
proud with its crisp bank and ditches
near Clun. It could keep cattle

in situ; not mock an army,
but hold a mere raider at bay.
I'm in the ditch, looking up
at that continuous bank,
steep, sharp, stopping the view;
have a dim idea how it feels

to be on top of it, proud.
Have had one foot in the ditch,
one on the bank, half my life.
So it goes on, goes up
and down, this Dyke, like my life,
out of Mynd, out of Clun.

1980   *Brian Louis Pearce*

CLIMBING THE LONG MYND

Close by a brook we made our way upstream
To the plash and gurgle of its downward bumble,
Ferns and late primroses grew along the tumble,
Dippers and wagtails fishing in the cream.
Up a steep lane we toiled in the hot sun
The banks on either side were deep and lush,
Waist high grasses frothed with parsley lace
Lady's smock and gems of vivid campion.

Out of the stifling heat we turned to seek
Rest and some shade within the bordering wood;
There washes of amethyst cooled our blood
An ocean of bluebells lapped about our feet.
Profusion of beauty where only chance may see?
Creation is content simply to be.

1988   *Mary Brett*

PLACE RHYMES

Stan upon Trent,
Stan upon Wye,
Clean Stan, dirty Stan,
And Stanton Lacy.

Trad.

Thrice happy be he
Between the Severn and the Clee.

Trad.

ON THE STIPERSTONES

These brooding crags, born in the remorseless grind
Of ice, have seen the Roman legions wind
Like ants across the Severn Plain below.
They saw proud Hotspur fall
At Shrewsbury, watched other princes come and go.
They've heard the battle call
Of Mercia and the wilder cries of Wales.
They whisper darker tales
Of deeds performed by Stone Age Man
Before our history began,
And through it all they've stayed remote,
Above the hunting birds which float
Below, planing in circles on the wind,
The neighbouring hills, the Wrekin and Long Mynd
Seem soft and kind, but here these castled stones
Protrude through Shropshire soil like shattered bones
Through torn flesh
Here Gog and Magog rest
Uneasily, and as both earth and thunder roll
Mere mortals hold a mirror to their soul.

1983   *Allister Fraser*

IN THE STRETTON HILLS

White clouds rolling, unfolding
Over cold blue spaces
Are glassed in the watery meadows.
White curls of lambs, new-dropped,
Pattern the weaning pastures
Crying to be succoured. The swollen streams
Trailing beaded curtains of weeping willow,
Flush the spring verges and draw in their foaming wakes
Freak winds from north and east.
Shafts of icy rain and grape-shot hail
Numb to stillness the vulnerable young;
Lambs, timid buds, and even the shielded sun
Arrested in winter's last clawing grasp.

But snowdrifts of blackthorn veil a cautious green;
Quivered arrows thrust, and helmeted buds,
Green whorls and cudgels, foetus flowers, press outwards.
They cover winter's retreat and shroud the dying
Of bracken, rusty and crushed, grey beards of grass,
And the wet, deep-layered leaf-lanes.

It is softening, sinking away, the finished season,
Returning to earth.
            A new generation, insidious, persistent,
Swings into the strong pulse-beat, the awesome rhythm
Of nature's established order.
Pray that no evil mutation
Of greater power will break this perfect circle.

1992   *Margery Lea*

HOPTON CASTLE

Rowan and elder
make a wild garden
here, grapple for light
at the austere

arches; ash-
saplings crane, crack stone
up the tiny crumbled stair.

This was a minor garrison
in empty hills, leaf-
crepitating: –
no prince, no belle dame.

But there was a siege
once, a betrayal,
a slaughter:
the moat water
holds they say old bones.

Under the weeping willows
the cattle drink
breast-metal, trothless irons.

1994   *V. Carlin*

LUDLOW
(from *The Worthiness of Wales*)

The Towne doth stand most part upon an Hill,
Built well and fayre, with streates both large and wide,
The houses such, where straungers lodge at will,
As long as there the councell lists abide,
Both fine and cleane the streates are all throughout,
With conduits cleere, and wholesome water springs;
And who that lists to walke the towne about,
But chiefly there the ayre so sweet you have,
As in no place ye can better crave...
Who doth beare sway, as turne doth come about,
Who chosen are, by oth and auncient guise.
Good lawes they have, and open space to pleade,
In ample sort, for right and Justice sake:
A Preacher too, that dayly there doth reade,
A Schoolemaster, that doth good schollers make.
And for the Queere, are boyes brought up to sing,
And to serve God, and doe none other thing.

1587   *Thomas Churchyard*

THE FIRST OF MAY

The orchards half the way
  From home to Ludlow fair
Flowered on the first of May
  In Mays when I was there;
And seen from style or turning
  The plume of smoke would show
Where fires were burning
  That went out long ago.

The plum broke forth in green,
  The pear stood high and snowed,
My friends and I between
  Would take the Ludlow road;
Dressed to the nines and drinking
  And light in heart and limb,
And each chap thinking
  The fair was held for him.

Between the trees in flower
  New friends at fairtime tread
The way where Ludlow tower
  Stands planted on the dead.
Our thoughts, a long while after,
  They think, our words they say;
Theirs now's the laughter,
  The fair, the first of May.

Ay, yonder lads are yet
  The fools that we were then;
For oh, the sons we get
  Are still the sons of men.
The sumless tale of sorrow
  Is all unrolled in vain:
May comes to-morrow
  And Ludlow fair again.

1922   *A.E. Housman*

SABRINA SINGS
(from 'Comus', first performed at Ludlow Castle in 1634*)*

By the rushy-fringed bank,
Where grows the willow and the osier dank,
  My sliding chariot stays,
Thick set with agate, and the azurn sheen
Of turkis blue, and emerald green,
  That in the channel strays:
Whilst from off the waters fleet
Thus I set my printless feet
O'er the cowslip's velvet head,
  That bends not as I tread.
Gentle swain, at thy request
  I am here!

1634   *John Milton*

LUDLOW REQUIEM

If you had lived, would you be with me now
Standing where once we stood so long ago?
Here in September's sun-ripe golden glow
Would we have kept our dew-kiss'd April vow?
Thro' magic woods where Comus worked his will,
Down sunlit paths that Philip Sidney knew,
By castle walls where once royal standards flew,
Over the years I wander with you still.
Then we knew beauty, youth and joy; of pain
Heedless were we, till war-clouds high above
Broke – and our hopes and dreams and you, my love,
Vanish'd away, and did not come again.
If you had lived, would our love-tale be told?
But you are gone: and I, alone, grow old.

1994   *Kathleen Collier*

SIGHT-SEEING

Ludlow is a must for solitary ladies.
They trudge purposefully
From street to street,
Some with cameras,
All with sensibly shod feet,
Absorbed by buildings,
Amazed at "black and white"
And Georgian vistas.

They peer through spectacles.
No smile escapes their lips
Hoping that tea
Will wash away their loneliness,
They make a bargain with a now
That promises a memory,
Carefully preserved,
Of happiness when they were here.

1994   *Patricia V. Dawson*

TOWARDS IT
(Ludlow)

and then the sun came out
through a crack
in the grey roofed sky
dripping tears of brightness
that burst like bubbles
across a black cloud
smudged landscape

yes

it's like graffiti
scrawled across a perfect memory

and, it begins
when you get to the Clee Hills
that's where it begins

and they stand there proudly
without regard for human beings

me

driving towards it
the hairs on my neck
prickling like a frightened cat's

me

inside the warm cab of my
pick up truck
36 monthly payments
through the nose

and it's
up and over
the bank

and a Baroque Sun
strengthening, spreading
opening a curtain of mist
that covers my Father's grave

but not St Lawrence's church
nor the castle
both are above the mist
standing like the hills

proudly without regard
for human beings

1984   *Mike Sargent*

THE VALLEY OF THE REA

The valley of the Rea is fair and wide,
  The gorse upon the upland is aglow;
And rolling pastures meet the riverside,
  Or cheery orchards blossom white as snow.

The cornfields (they are scattered here and there
  As if by chance they fell from out the sky),
Give promise of a crop both rich and rare,
  Their tender shoots like bright green carpets lie.

On mossy banks the ferns and violets grow
  And dew-damp clusters of the bright primrose;
Tall foxgloves nod their heads when breezes blow,
  But queen of every hedgerow is the rose.

The ever flowing River babbles on,
  The open-reaches glint beneath the sun;
Now into leafy caverns she has gone,
  And over stony fords she gaily runs.

At Reaside Farm which once was Cromwell's seat,
  Forgotten is the ringing clash of arms;
Now calves do softly call and lambs do bleat,
  And happy children play about the barns.

The white-faced cattle stare with wondering eye,
  A lazy crane sails idly o'er the stream;
The curly-coated sheep with timid eye,
  Of these, when far away, a man may dream.

Early 20th C.   *Simon Evans*
          (The poet postman of Cleobury Mortimer)

FARLOW

"Hlūde waeron hȳ, lā hlūde, thā hȳ ofer thone hlāēw ridan." – *Old English Charm*

As the swishing of the cycle-wheels rebounded in the arch
Of hazelnutted hedges left too long untrimmed,
Up and down the marl, O strong unshiny rims,
In the brook-dissected country of the green Salopian March,
My brother and I in the smothered copses
Passed many a hamlet on the clay-ridge tops.

As the bikes were like a vessel in the growths of vegetation,
In the rolling wooded landscape, in the pieced and peaceful fields,
We stopped their chains a while, and a silence ears could feel
With a pulsing hard sensation, in the moment's hesitation,
Reinforced the green impression of the middles of the lanes,
Through the tar all rank the grasses, to our city-eyes so strange.

And so we came to Farlow in high summer '64,
Two bikes with boys from Birmingham, who tracked the feet of Clee,
Where the reddish humps that slumber there are undesigned and free,
And the weekend-cottaged landscape all a shaggy foliage wore:
In the little shop we lingered, longed in lightness to dissolve
In the hedges tall and plaited and the silence that they wove.

1986   *Joseph Biddulph*

BLOWN CLEE
(from *Two Old Battered Caravans*)

Blow wind, in your persistence, and shake the trees
That clatter in the wood on Brown Clee Hill;
The storm rises now, pushing down the flue
The wood-smoke and stovesi-smoke, to taint the 'van:
Go, shake us, wind from Wales, crack us if you can –
Our mild steel frame, admittedly, 's not new,
But in its quarter-century no ill
Has holed the home that trembles in your breeze,

O rough Atlantic storm! Wind has a smell,
A smell of smoke, a little sharp, but quaint:
the night that daily round us puts a cloak
Of silence, sings this night with buffetings,
And in squalls the stove flares, and sings –
Suddenly the quiet world awoke,
And oval Brown Clee in its sea of red paint –
The tawny mud – shuddered with your spell.

O here is the quiet joy and happiness!
For, even if I wonder if I need
To stagger in the dark and rope us down,
The smell of rural night will wrap my clothes
In beech and oak, and stranger scents than those,
And distant lights are all I see of town:
Somehow, in your dashing squalls, I'm freed,
And feel a tender aim in our distress:

A vital being-human in the wood,
A oneness with the wind our fathers knew,
A consolation, unexpected, true,
A resurrected confidence of good.

Blow, wind, and shake the shock-budded birch
That purples on the slope of Brown Clee Hill,
And never let me lose your breath of good!
Wave pastures, and assault the standing dead bracken,
Pour your streams in teems, and never slacken
Your sense of oneness in the bending wood:
Welcome to your coldness! Welcome to you still!
Like Holy Ghost that blows to cheer the Church!

Come, let the 'van be gently tossed
And sway in the play of your fine Pentecost!

1986   *Joseph Biddulph*

from
THE ENGLISH VILLAGE
(Quatford)

You see yon Castle strong and high,

Looking in pride upon the vale below,
Where Severn through enamelled meads doth flow,
Around it myriad Roses thickly spring
In lengthened avenue and fairy ring,
As though 'twere Nature's first and favorite bower
Raised by her mandate in some joyful hour;
Here in past times was spread a barren moor,
A hopeless waste, shunned both by rich and poor,
With not a blade to bless the aching sight,
Cursed it was said by an enduring blight;
And thus for many centuries it lay
A sad memento of unchecked decay...

1859   *George Griffith*

THE SEVERN

Sweet on the margin of the Severn's stream,
  Where the green lime in summer time is drooping,
  And on the daisy-printed meadow sloping,
Blessing, descends the breeze, and morning beam!
Or in the ruins of some olden fane.
  Marking its dim and ivy-mantled way,
Where generations now serene are sleeping;
  And reigns supreme with undisputed sway
The Raven who has long his warder-watch been keeping.

19th C   *David Simons*

PRINCESS ETHELFLEDA, THE LADY OF MERCIA

Glorious Elfleda, born to victory,
The masterpiece of Nature shines in thee!
Thy outward form for beauty was designed,
But Heaven informed thee with a manly mind:
The virtues of both sex in thee are seen –
A king in fact, though a vicegerent queen.
Caesar the conquered world subdued; but thou
Would'st make the conqueror himself to bow!

12th C   *Henry of Huntingdon*

Princess Ethelfleda, the daughter of King Alfred, fortified a site where Bridgnorth
now stands.

EPITAPH ON FRANCIS MOORE

Here, five foot deep, lies on his back
A cobbler, starmonger and quack,
Who to the stars in pure goodwill
Does to his best look upward still.
Weep all ye customers who use
His pills, his almanacs, or his shoes.

18th C   *Jonathan Swift*

Francis Moore, original compiler of the famous *Old Moore's Almanac*, was born in
Bridgnorth in 1657.

from
CORVE DALE

Beneath the shade of Wenlock edge,
Where Corve in deeper shadow runs
And warblers pipe among the sedge
Their lazy notes, I stumbled once
Upon a sleepy hamlet, dozing
In the self-same sun that shone
When, within this vale reposing,
Basked the sons of Uricon.
Then a shambles, where the Roman
Proud beneath the eagle's wings
Drove the sturdy British foeman
From beside his native springs;
Now you show no sign of battle;-
Kindly earth has smoothed the dyke
Into pastures, where the cattle
Browse, and where the hungry shrike
Hymns his shard-winged victim ere he strike.
The eagled standard crumbles and decays;
Forgotten are the old, imperial days.
But Corve flows on, and quiet to the sky
The peaceful fields and ancient forests lie....

1920   *Hugh Ferley*

from
THE WORFIELD BELLS

Sweet village bells! sweet village bells!
How many a tale your music tells!
And as the gales your soft notes borrow,
They waft me much of joy and sorrow.
When first I heard your soothing chime
My life and hopes were in their prime,
And, full of joy and youthful glee,
Your music brought no pang to me;
But now ye tell another tale,
Loading with sad lament the gale,
And speak in accents soft and slow
How vain, how fragile all below!
But see, thro' azure towering high
Yon peaceful spire ascends the sky!

1822   *Catherine Bache*

from
A SHROPSHIRE LAD (XXXI)

On Wenlock Edge the wood's in trouble;
  His forest fleece the Wrekin heaves;
The gale, it plies the saplings double,
  And thick on Severn snow the leaves.

'Twould blow like this through holt and hanger
  When Uricon the city stood:
'Tis the old wind in the old anger,
  But then it threshed another wood.

Then, 'twas before my time, the Roman
  At yonder heaving hill would stare:
The blood that warms an English yeoman,
  The thoughts that hurt him, they were there.

There, like the wind through woods in riot,
  Through him the gale of life blew high;
The tree of man was never quiet:
  Then 'twas the Roman, now 'tis I.

The gale, it plies the saplings double,
  It blows so hard, 'twill soon be gone:
To-day the Roman and his trouble
  Are ashes under Uricon.

1896   *A.E. Housman*

from
A SHROPSHIRE LAD (XXXIX)

'Tis time, I think, by Wenlock town
  The golden broom should blow;
The hawthorn sprinkled up and down
  Should charge the land with snow.

Spring will not wait the loiterer's time
  Who keeps so long away;
So others wear the broom and climb
  The hedgerows heaped with may.

Oh tarnish late on Wenlock Edge,
  Gold that I never see;
Lie long, high snowdrifts in the hedge
  That will not shower on me.

1896   *A.E. Housman*

PRIORY RUINS, MUCH WENLOCK

pale roses cloistered
where white robed doves
inhabit high corridors

petal fragments fallen
in the transept
like lost psalms

my soul responds, dilates
seeing you there
in the green nave
holding a white rose
pure as Shropshire air

1994   *Gladys Mary Coles*

from
A SONG OF THE CHASE
(Willey)

Salopians every one,
Of high and low degree,
Who take delight in fox-hunting,
Come listen unto me.

A story true I'll tell to you
Concerning of a fox,
How they hunted him on Tickwood side
O'er Benthall Edge and rocks.

Says Reynard, "I'll take you o'er to Willey Park
Above there, for when we fairly get aground
I value neither huntsmen all
Nor Squire Forester's best hound.

I know your dogs are stout and good,
That they'll run me like the wind!
But I'll tread lightly on the land,
And leave no scent behind."

18th C   *Anon*

AUTUMN, WILLEY PARK

Now dew lies heavy on the ailing grass
And rimes the regimented gloom of fir;
Undressing hedgerows blush one final tint
Where wings of summer's insects vainly stir
Through mystic contours of the carriage drive
To fail and fall in laps of sleeping trees
Whose boughs peruse the rhododendron buds,
While winter poisons each successive breeze.
Uncertain ardour shelters where it may
And ripened pheasant tempts the gamesman's gun;
A nervous rabbit drums its morning beat;
A vixen marks her last permitted run.

Here, to my hidden vantage, flocking sheep
Come down. Their ease sits well about the Hall
And complements its noble heritage
With a more humble, more pacific call.
Such is this crucible of magic brushed
By peacefulness denouncing ravaged years
Where lilies on the lake string gossamer
That threads the soul of England through with tears.

1994   *John Roughton*

SONNET TO COLEBROOKE DALE

Thy Genius, Colebrooke, faithless to his charge
Amid thy woods and vales, thy rocks and streams,
Formed for the train that haunt poetic dreams,
Naiads and nymphs, – now hears the toiling barge
And the swart Cyclops' ever-changing forge
Din in thy dells; – permits the dark-red gleams,
From umbered fires on all thy hills, the beams,
Solar and pure, to shroud with columns large
Of black sulphureous smoke, that spread their veils
Like funeral crape upon the sylvan robe
Of thy romantic rocks, pollute thy gales,
And stain thy glassy floods; – while o'er the globe
To spread thy stores metallic, this rude yell
Drowns the wild woodland song, and breaks the Poet's spell.

1799   *Anna Seward*

THE SHROPSHIRE IRONMASTER
(John Wilkinson)

Before I proceed with my lingo
You shall all drink my toast in a bumper of stingo.
Fill up, and without any further parade,
John Wilkinson, boys, the supporter of trade.

May all his endeavours be crowned with success
And his works ever growing prosperity bless.
May his comforts increase with the length of his days
And his fame shine as bright as his furnace's blaze.

That the wood of old England would fail, did appear,
And tho' iron was scarce because charcoal was dear,
By puddling and stamping he cured that evil,
So the Swedes and the Russians may go to the devil.

Our thundering cannon, too frequently burst,
As mischief so great he prevented the first,
And now it is well known they never miscarry
But drive on our foes with a blast of Old Harry.

Then let each jolly fellow take hold of his glass
And drink to the health of his friend and his lass.
May we always have plenty of stingo and pence,
And Wilkinson's flame blaze a thousand years hence.

19th C   *Anon*

SHROPSHIRE VALE
(Ironbridge)

In the vale
was the red unholy fire –
the river imaging the everchanging
colour as the sparks fell in burning showers
while men sweated and cursed
at the furnace mouth pungent with odours,
sulphurous and choking, bringing that fierce
amalgam of ore and coking coal
to fashion those gates of heaven and
the iron bridge to span the eternal river...

Today in this vale
and among remembered hills, they salute
the ghosts of past industrial glories –
Factories that were fabricated in a dream,
now come alive, burning with a bright colour
clinging in custom-built style to a patient landscape
where modern "toilers" in air-conditioned place employ
slip-stream techniques to fashion futuristic parts
quicker than the batting of an eye.

But at the end it is...
the trial and error, blood and bone, iron
in the soul that form a weld bringing together
purpose and people of different nations, joined
in a great endeavour to create
fresh visions in the vale...

1994   *Wrathall K. Wildman*

COALBROOKDALE

Profuse in crevices
a mayweed's yellow eye peers
from the rock. Pink snapdragon
sticks out and travellers' joy
tumbles in falling star-trek
over old high walls. Here
in a wasteland of derelict furnaces
where polished berries, scarlet, green
twine bryony-wise among pale crumbling brick
history clings
close as a stonecrop carpet
lavish in August sun.

Once in this rustic waste
invention stirred. The valley tense
with noise, industry
swift as a spring tide surged
through Severn gorge. By night
flame lit the plangent sky. Huge clouds
of dust rose, mushroomed over trees. Vessel
wharf, warehouse looming large
filled up with intricate castings
iron art.
The metal bloom, inferno, ships
are gone. All that now ravels silence
in this sylvan place
cool-caverned, blue in fluent dash below
the old wheel-race.

1972   *M.A.B. Jones*

TO BUILDWAS BRIDGE BY SEVERNSIDE

So long ago and yet it seems but yesterday!
The three of us would wend our way
Through Coalbrookdale to Severnside,
Where here and there a boat would glide
To lend enchantment to the scene.

Here we would pause and dream,
Then take the narrow path that leads
Along the bank where dragonflies – like small mosaic pieces,
In mid-air –softly dart.

By the fringed path we wandered
Nor turned aside until we reached
The Buildwas bridge and road to Wenlock town;
Up hill then down along a peaceful country road
Where tranquil brooklet flows all bordered by a grey stone wall.

Here – loveliest sight of all –
A wide green verge on either side
Lay thick with violets, blue and white,
Whose colour far outvies the pale forget-me-not.

Untroubled by the sound of wheels
All heedless of the time that steals
Upon us in this dear familiar place,
We find that we must mend our pace.

See, darkling clouds foretell the rain
And we must catch the Severn Valley train.

1962   *Gwen Simmonds*

THOUGHTS AT BUILDWAS ABBEY

Cloister-cool the walls
like crumbling lava turned to stone.
Religion has cooled and frozen
in the ruined monastic maze.

The wind drifts by in thistledown
like a silken priest's robe.
On my bare legs
the hot rush of sun
in the earth-filled chapel –
it seems like the grave of faith:

yet the memory is alive in dead stone.
People pay through ticket barriers;
plans explain the rooms
once filled with learned monks.
The chapter house holds a glazed tile patch;
the Treasury holds a cart and a sleeping bat
like a monk, cloistered, asleep in his faith –

I prod it and it rises like a ghost
vanishing into rafters but leaving
no unturned gold behind.
Drizzle falls and emptiness creeps in;
mole-hills have invaded, undermining –
the faith and monks both gone.
But brown-clad creatures still rummage
heedless to anyone's calls.

I too run outside the walls, having tunnelled
inside. Now the lane lies before me.
I'll come again in June
when swallows have nested everywhere
and the daisies live in the mole-hills.
Weeds wetten the ruins
but Nature's faith is always renewed.

1994   *Ceri Courtenay*

from
POLYOLBION

The haughty Cambrian Hills enamor'd of their praise
(As they who onely sought ambitiously to raise
The blood of god-like Brute) their heads do proudly beare:
And having crown'd themselves sole Regents of the Ayre
(An other warre with Heaven as though they meant to make)
Did seeme in great disdaine the bold affront to take,
That any petty hill upon the English side,
Should dare, not (with a crouch) to vale unto their pride.

When Wrekin, as a hill his proper worth that knew,
And understood from whence their insolencie grew,
For all that they appear'd so terrible in sight,
Yet would not once forgoe a jote that was his right.
And when they star'd on him, to them the like he gave,
And answer'd glance for glance, and brave againe for brave:
That, when some other hills which English dwellers were,
The lustie Wrekin saw himselfe so well to beare
Against the Cambrian part, respectless of their power.

1622   *Michael Drayton*

from
THE ARMADA

The Wrekin was a link in the chain of beacon fires lit to warn of the
sighting of the Spanish Armada in 1588.

All night from tower to tower they sprang:
  they sprang from hill to hill:
Till the proud Peak unfurled the flag o'er
  Darwin's rocky dales,
Till like volcanoes flared to heaven the stormy
  hills of Wales,
Till twelve fair counties saw the blaze on
  Malvern's lonely height,
Till streamed in crimson on the wind the Wrekin's
  crest of light...

1842/3   *Lord Macaulay*

FROM ADMASTON

There was a time I yet remember well,
When oft I've heard the weary reapers tell,
That when at even the Wreken's top was clear,
Serene and bright the morning would appear,
But when dark clouds his summit should deform,
The day succeeding ever brought a storm:
And many an hour, by murm'ring brook or rill,
I've pensive marked the distant Wreken hill,
What time the ev'ning sun declin'd to rest,
And ruddy streaks have ting'd the peaceful west;
Then homeward have I bent my lonely way,
Musing, prophetic, on the coming day.

1814   *Charles B. Ash*

LIMERICK

There was an Old Man of the Wrekin
Whose shoes made a horrible creaking
But they said, "Tell us whether, your shoes are of leather,
Or of what, you Old Man of the Wrekin?"

1846   *Edward Lear*

THE WREKIN

Driving to meet
my children from
school and seeing
a fat, red sun
straddle The Wrekin,
I know why old
religions take nature
for their god.

Two tractors, great,
green John Deere
machines close to,
seen from the lane
are pocket-sized
as they redesign
the hill to
Wrockwardine.

I park outside
the shop
and, leaving doors
unlocked, lean on
the Church Farm wall
and watch a turkey
and a peacock
squaring-up,
while waiting
for school to end.

Friends in Telford,
from Japan,
talk at length about
Mount Fujisan
and how uplifting
a hill can be.
I understand.
The Wrekin does the
same for me.

1994   *Jim Hatfield*

from
URICONIUM

It lieth low near merry England's heart
Like a long-buried sin; and Englishmen
Forget that in its death their sires had part.
And, like a sin, Time lays it bare again
   To tell of races wronged,
And ancient glories suddenly overcast,
And treasures flung to fire and rabble wrath.
   If thou hast ever longed
To lift the gloomy curtain of Time Past,
And spy the secret things that Hades hath,
Here through this riven ground take such a view.
The dust, that fell unnoted as a dew,
Wrapped the dead city's face like a mummy-cloth:
All is as was: except for worm and moth.

Since Jove was worshipped under Wrekin's shade
Or Latin phrase was writ in Shropshire stone,
Since Druid chaunts desponded in this glade
Or Tuscan general called that field his own,
   How long ago? How long?
How long since wanderers in the Stretton Hills
Met men of shaggy hair and savage jaw,
   With flint and copper prong,
Aiming behind their dikes and thorny grilles?
    Ah! those were days before the axe and saw,
    Then were the nights when this mid-forest town
    Held breath to hear the wolves come yelping down,
    And ponderous bears 'long Severn lifted paw,
    And nuzzling boars ran grunting through the shaw.

1913 (pub 1983)   *Wilfred Owen*

KRISTIANI AT VIROCONIUM

Each summer we would go out, my son;
no, not we citizens, but the Imperial Army,
cohort upon cohort, splendidly equipped
and drilled to perfection, a sight indeed to see,
like many sights which lie in ruin now.
We would go out and fight the barbarians.
Always we won.
We brought their leaders to the forum there
to bend beneath the yoke in servitude...
yonder, where the fallen arch is now,
where purple weeds cover the fractured plinth,
the very plinth on which an Emperor once stood.
Those of us who read the old lettering still
can tell you the wording there. It marked his rank
and reads...but what's the use?
You would not understand.
Your eyes reflect an emptiness
that's more profound than all the old philosophy.
My only comfort now is that
your ignorance will never feel the bitter
gall of folly our old knowledge brought.
"Barbarians?" you ask. "Who are they?"
They are us, my son, ourselves.
Did we but know we put ourselves
beneath the yoke each summer
that we brought our treasure home.
We spoiled ourselves with wealth and greed;
for in the summer that the Empire fell
there came confusion, disbelief.
That one summer we did not go out
to fight, but stayed at home in ease
watching the army march away for good,
the barbarians came to us instead.

We always knew they would, those of us
who saw the signs within ourselves.
They came in wild, unbridled hordes,
screaming undisciplined cries, crudely
undrilled and ragged, yet murderously efficient.
We were no match for them,
too far gone in sweet and easy living.
We fled who could and hid.
We left the city and the villa where they stood.
We left our household gods; or rather, so it seems,
our gods deserted us.
We had to learn afresh through pain,
through penury, through death,
of all the old life meant to us.
Our new life lies within the orbit
of this ring I wear, the fish-ring
given by the Greek who traded
wine for years with us.
It will be recognised, he said, by those we seek
far in the west who hide out there.
He spoke of another Life, another Kingdom;
practised strange rites with bread and wine
he and his family; spoke words of prophecy and hope.
There are others of his creed high in the hills
and further west across the sea, scattered.
They alone hold fast to what is best,
better far than all we lost.
And that is why we come to look our last,
before we start our journey in the dawn;
begin again our search for truth and life –
this time through Christ.

1974   *John Waddington-Feather*

Viroconium, a Roman city in Shropshire, was abandoned by the Romano-British after the
collapse of the Roman Empire in the 5th century AD. Colonies of Christians established
settlements in remote places further west in Wales and in Ireland to avoid attack by
pagans.

VIROCONIUM

Virocon – Virocon –
Still the ancient name rings on
And brings, in the untrampled wheat,
The tumult of a thousand feet.

Where trumpets rang and men marched by,
None passes but the dragon-fly.
Athwart the grassy town, forlorn,
The lone dor-beetle blows his horn.

The poppy standards droop and fall
Above one rent and mournful wall:
In every sunset-flame it burns,
Yet towers unscathed when day returns.

And still the breaking seas of grain
Flow havenless across the plain:
The years wash on, their spindrift leaps
Where the old city, dreaming, sleeps.

Grief lingers here, like mists that lie
Across the dawns of ripe July;
On capital and corridor
The pathos of the conqueror.

The pillars stand, with alien grace,
In churches of a younger race;
The chiselled column, black and rough,
Becomes a roadside cattle-trough:

The skulls of men who, right or wrong,
Still wore the splendour of the strong,
Are shepherds' lanterns now, and shield
Their candles in the lambing field.

But when, through evening's open door,
Two lovers tread the broken floor,
And the wild-apple petals fall
Round passion's scarlet festival;

When cuckoos call from the green gloom
Where dark, shelving forests loom;
When foxes bark beside the gate,
And the grey badger seeks his mate –

There haunts within them secretly
One that lives while empires die,
A shrineless god whose songs abide
Forever in the countryside.

1924   *Mary Webb*

PRESENCES
(Lyth Hill)

There is a presence on the lonely hill,
Lovely and chill:
There is an emanation in the wood,
Half understood.
They come upon me like an evening cloud
Stranger than moon-rise, whiter than a shroud.
I shall not see them plain
Ever again,
Though in my childhood days
I knew their ways.
They are as secret as the black cloud-shadows
Sliding along the ripe midsummer grass;
With a breath-taking majesty they pass,
Down by the water in the mournful meadows;
Out of the pale pink distance at the falling
Of dusk they gaze – remote, summoning, chill;
Sweetly in April I have heard them calling
Where through black ash-buds gleams the purple hill.

1924   *Mary Webb*

THE LITTLE HILL
(Pontesford)

This is the hill, ringed by the misty shire –
The mossy, southern hill,
The little hill where larches climb so high.
Among the stars aslant
They chant;
Along the purple lower slopes they lie
In lazy golden smoke, more faint, more still
Than the pale woodsmoke of the cottage fire.
Here some calm Presence takes me by the hand
And all my heart is lifted by the chant
Of them that lean aslant
In golden smoke and sing, and softly bend:
And out from every larch-bole steals a friend.

1924   *Mary Webb*

LYTH BANK
(October 1979)

Where are you now
Berry-brown lady
Who lived and loved her days
In this forsaken corner of the scented woods
Beloved by nature's beings?
Within this secret, shy cottage
You thought of cherished family times
Before the gradual dawning
Of the ever-present abandonment,
And found your consolation
In this same scene of Exfords Green
And Annscroft just across the pastures' view.
Are you today imprisoned in the threatened
Brick-bound streets
Whose urban shadows tinted sadness
In those kindly eyes of yours,
Longing to hear your banished-vanished
Terrier's keen yapping
At this garden gate
Where I the wandering stranger paused
To share some moments of your quiet days
And with you look down upon
The lanes of your life
The fields of your life
The hills of your life.

I see them now
Through the shock-jagged panes
Of the cottage of your life.
But where are you, berry-brown lady
Of yesterday's past?

1994   *Margaret Austin*

Lyth Bank is situated just below Mary Webb's old home at Spring Cottage

BOMERE POOL
(to Mary Webb)

Rings of aged bark
conceal this dark mere,
recipient of life;

muted, the bells in its core
unsounded, drowned
with the village, lost
in the swallowing well
unfathomable as the black hole
of a collapsed star.

Linked trees hold
the spell:
tall lichened alchemists
distilling a special silence,
permitting particular sounds.

Listen! You might hear
the breath of time

whispered in the sipping
of the mere, liquid lips
incessant
to the dipped boughs;
echoed in rooks' raw cries,
contractions of pathos
answered by the bittern
or a solitary heron
objectively fashioning
its reflection;

and ever the hint
of leaf music,
soundless sigh of roots,
mashy moist of earth
becoming mud,
dispersing.

1994   Gladys Mary Coles

PENDULUM

They have tidied up the mere,
Mary Webb,
Tidied the mere.
You might feel disappointed,
Mary Webb,
Crave the forsaken jungle
Of your day
If you were here.

Rush rhododendron
Thicket marsh and fern
Are scant in girth and number,
Or are gone.
To landing jetty
Pleasure boats
And buoy
Time has marched on.

The boat house,
Fully licensed,
A-la-carte,
Provides a first-class luncheon
In the bar.
The pathways to the waterline are clear
And (need one add)
Give access for the car.

What do you ask,
Strange woman of the mist?
Oh no – good gracious no!
We motored down.
We've had the lunch
And a post-prandial drink,
And may stroll out
Before we drive to town.

Oh, don't go on so, Mary!
All's not lost,
Your joyous gloom
Begot our gloomy gift,
And I suspect,
If you were here today
You'd not refuse the dinner,
Or the lift.

1994   *Peter Gate*

(Awarded second prize, Wrekin Writers Open Poetry Competition, 1990)

SHREWSBURY
(from *The Worthiness of Wales*)

Three gates there are through which you needes must passe,
   As to the heights of towne the people goe:
So Castle seemes as 'twere a looking glasse,
To look through all, and hold them all in awe;
Treangle-wise the gates and towne doth drawe:
But Castle Hyll spyes out each streete so plaine,
As though an eye on them did still remaine.
About the walles, trim under goodly banks,
   Doth Severne passe, and comes by Cotton Hill:
Much praise they had, and purchast many thanks,
   That at Stonebridge make place for many a mill.

Full from Welshbridge, alone by meddowes greene,
   The river runs, most fayre and fine to vewe;
Such fruitfull ground as this is seldome seene
   In many parts, if that I hear be true.

Yet each man knowes that grasse is in his pride,
And ayre is fresh by every rivers side;
But sure this plot doth farre surpasse the rest,
That by good lot is by the graces blest.

Who hath desire to vewe both hill and vale,
Walke up old wall, of castle rude and bare,
And he shall see such pleasure set to sale,
   In kindly sort, as though some merchants ware
Were set in shop to please the passer by;
Or els by shewe beguyld the gazers eye;
For look but downe along the pleasant coast,
And he shall thank his labour is not lost.

One way appears Stonebridge and subbarbs there,
   Which called is the Abbey forehed yet:
A long great streate, well-builded, large and faire,
   In as good ayre as any may be wisht with wit:
Where Abbey stands, and is such ring of belles
As is not found from London unto Welles:
   The steeple yet a gracious pardon findes,
To bide all blasts, all weathers, stormes, and windes...

1587   *Thomas Churchyard*

BATTLE OF SHREWSBURY

        Why is Rumour here?
I run before King Harry's victory;
Who, in a bloody field by Shrewsbury,
Hath beaten down young Hotspur and his troops,
Quenching the flame of bold rebellion
Even with the rebel's blood. But what mean I
To speak so true at first? my office is
To noise abroad that Harry Monmouth fell
Under the wrath of noble Hotspur's sword;
And that the king before the Douglas' rage
Stoop'd his anointed head as low as death.
This have I rumour'd through the peasant towns
Between that royal field of Shrewsbury
And this worm-eaten hold of ragged stone,
Where Hotspur's father, old Northumberland,
Lies crafty-sick: the posts come tiring on,
And not a man of them brings other news
Than they have learn'd of me: from Rumour's tongues
They bring smooth comforts false, worse than true wrongs.

1600   *William Shakespeare*

ABBEY
(Shrewsbury)

With fine brook, fish-filtering,
fertile land, grapes ripening,
the place, prime when summer-flush
steadied Severn's spring-spate rush,
Benedictine's rich city
served many a century.

Living its tally of days
unending paean of praise,
there was room for work, study,
solemn vigil in Abbey
with colour-blaze, song sublime,
great state at festival-time.

Spot chosen by river-edge,
fair with pink willow-herb, sedge,
clustered under the high crown
of this bustling Border-town,
its household furnished good life,
sanctuary from the world's strife.

A road now over the site,
darkness and silence by light
and traffic-glare are replaced –
history barely to be traced,
and crowds at the Foregate heart
blind to the place set apart:
Refectory Lectern, last
legacy of a lost past.

1988   *M.A.B. Jones*

(In Welsh metre, read at the Abbey Flower Festival, September 1990)

SHREWSBURY: 1916

Lassoed by Severn, all hills, half-timber.
One bridge lilted as they crossed;
another spoke stone dolphins.
The Infirmary hung sheer as the castle,
a cliff of balconies, chest-cases.
Spires braced them, under blue arc-lamps
shunting – engines coughed them to the brink –
the bread-biting, glinty minnows.
They return as boys, ignoring
the swans that ignored them,
belting a half-squashed football,
coats for posts.

1978   *Geoffrey Holloway*

BY SALOP WEIR, SHREWSBURY

Shadow lengthened into darkness
Fingering the town
And made that island ours.
We took the old steps
Under castle walls, below
The railbridge, by the prison;
The moon had a wry smile
For tentative friends
Kissing answers
Their innocence thought true
And a melt of needing
Held this moment,
Made it a memory to keep
Against the cold indifference
that followed in a week or two.

The spate by the weir
Crows of loves
Beginning, ending here
Where tow-path lamps
Glitter rings of water;
Generations step down
Hand-in-hand by the oracle
And the Severn's sadness
Winds the trysting ribbon round.

1994   *John Roughton*

RIVER SEVERN AT SHREWSBURY

A sharpie
Skilfully displayed
At bridge level
To split the water
Pulls up fast
Then another
To take over
– Commands shouted from the bank
Astride a bicycle

A single Canada goose
Off earth –
Hope singing

Two mallards
Cover the river
Then under the bridge
At daring speed

Daffodils blaze out
Breaking through
Clean cut on the river banks

Games of bowls going on
By floodlight
Voices persevere
Over the hedge
Into the wind

Two Springer spaniels
With a garrulous owner
Both sticking it out

The crack of wings
Fighting with foliage
For release

All kinds of duck and antics
On the river
In this disparate time of year

Sheep and a single cry
From a flock
Low grounded at the water
A luminous sky
Pale grey, dark edged
Going on to colour
And full of life

Against the dark
The houses ever mount
Their show of light
And climb upon the river bank,
Down at its edge
That one animal cry

An excited bird in the half-light
Saying
"This is just the beginning"

Off the river
A sweet and lovely boy
With hemiplegia
Told me the way to the castle
Looking back, he said
– "I hope you find it"

1988   *Roy Batt*

SEVERN MINNOWS

In the sun's strobe their quick silver
looks random as spilt nails –
yet each moves with acute control;
never touching, however curt
the space between.

They were the totems, devout joys
of my Shropshire childhood:
inches of glory risen
from pouncy nets and half sunk jars
to glittered sills.

"They won't keep, you know" said grownups.
I used to try, four days –
but could never win, before time
unforgivably some white gut
would surface, stop.

They were here when the troop trains went:
shoals flashing bayonets –
when the spare, khaki ghosts slopped back,
in and out of their smashed, wet skulls
like loose shrapnel.

They are here now, in the Bren's brisk
tock from Copthorne Barracks
– sound of a butcher chopping meat –
with no swans, only a river
lead-ripped, sad.

1982   *Geoffrey Holloway*

THE QUARRY THEATRE IN SHREWSBURY
(from *The Worthiness of Wales*)

Behind the walles as chiefe
Where playes have bin, which is most worthie note,
There is a ground, newe made theator wise,
Bothe deepe and hye, in goodly auncient guise,
Where well may sit, ten thousand men at ease,
And yet the one, the other not displease.

A space belowe, to bayte both bull and beare,
For players too, great roume and place at will,
And in the same, a cocke pit wondrous feare:
Besides where men, may wrastle in their fill.
A ground most apt, and they that sits above,
At once in vewe, all this may see for love:
At Aston's play, who had beheld this then,
Might well have seene, there twentie thousand men!

1587   *Thomas Churchyard*

ROUNDEL

In Shrewsbury Town e'en Hercules wox tired,
Tired of the streets that end not up nor down;
Tired of the Quarry, though seats may be hired
Of Shrewsbury Town.

Tired of the tongues that knew not his renown;
Tired of the Quarry Bye-Laws, so admired
By the Salopian, the somnambulant clown.

Weak as a babe, and in like wise attired,
He leaned upon his club; frowned a last frown,
And of ineffable boredom, so expired.
In Shrewsbury Town.

1917 (pub 1983)   *Wilfred Owen*

from
SHREWSBURY QUARRY

The Shrewsbury Show described here was held in the same area as the present Shrewsbury Flower Show and was doubtless a forerunner to it.

What friendly forms in social pomp draw near,
With thankful smiles to bless the bounteous year!
In glad procession, brotherhood, and bloom,
(Like *Flora's* festals near thy walls, oh Rome,)
The bands distinguished, yet harmonious move,
Their ensigns concord, and their leaders love;
To KINGSLAND'S Arbours once a year they go,
In ordered elegance serene and slow;
The Bodies Corporate in classes bright –
In different classes, but in one delight;
There blend with mutual hands the friendly bowls,
There blend their wishes and there blend their souls;
The yearly *Archon* over all presides,
Their state he governs and their joy he guides,
There mixing jovial with each jovial band,
To each he gives his heart – to each his hand;
With each he quaffs the invigorating cheer,
To friendship sacred, and the hallow'd year;
There union, brotherhood, and mirth combine,
In every face these vital virtues shine.

18th C   *Anon*

ON THE DEATH OF SIR PHILIP SIDNEY

Two lines written on the death of his friend and fellow pupil at Shrewsbury School

Knowledge his light hath lost, Valour hath slain her knight,
Sidney is dead, dead is my friend, dead is the world's delight.

16th C   *Fulke Greville*

THE AVENUE OF LIMES
(Shrewsbury Quarry)

The avenue of limes was old
When we were young.
We mourned their felling
One by crashing one.
Sad and bare
The air bereft of scent,
"It would never be the same,"
We said.
"The spindly striplings
Planted in the gaps
Would never grow to full maturity."

Walking on an evening, after rain,
We were suddenly aware
Of refreshing perfume
Hanging in the air.
Looking up we saw
The once raw trees
Grown lush and vibrant green.
The avenue of limes is young,
We are old.

1994   Margaret Colledge

FELLOW TOWNSMAN
(Written on the terrace of Shrewsbury Library)

A sense of fellowship
Warms my Salopian frame
As I sit here
In the shadow
Of the statue
Of Charles Darwin.

Darwin was born on what we call The Mount –
I was born on the Mount!

The Severn dawdled almost past his garden –
It meandered through my childhood.

The shuts and alleys of old Salop knew his footsteps –
that same old honeycomb was home to me.

Publicly modest, privately quite vain –
I share his weakness and his secret guilt.

Of like physique, environment and hope –
What end to this enthralling enterprise?
Darwin had a beard –
I have a beard!

Darwin wrote the Origin of the Species.

I, too, was born on the Mount.

1984   *Peter Gate*

SHREWSBURY PEOPLE

are so different,
she said,
on returning from
dining and dancing
to a six piece band
at a three star hotel
on the bypass.
They are so...,
she struggled for the
word, different.

Mmm, the babysitter
replied, without
conviction. The word
she sought was
cosmopolitan. Here,
meaning Clun, she went
on, everyone is
identical. Same clothes,
same ideas, same
everything. But there,
meaning Shrewsbury,
everybody is, well,
different.

The babysitter kept
mum. Glad to be where
he was after years of
city living, he'd
had a bellyfull of
cosmopolis. Clun suited
him. He found it different.

1989   *Jim Hatfield*

DRESS SENSE

You should have had more glitter
on your Caribbean cruise, you told us,
and more stylish shoes to match the clientele.
My friend, amused, said:
"Don't bring your sequins up to Shrewsbury."

You may need something neat
in a West End London street
with your artistes' club and concerts
and bright lights or when you take
the stage to play or sing – but
don't take your sequins up to Shrewsbury.

When you're tramping the Long Mynd
in an unforgiving wind
or laden down with shopping on the bus
you're better with strong shoes,
a storm-proof mac and old rucksack,
so don't take your sequins up to Shrewsbury.

1991   *Margaret Caunt*

WILLIAM WICHERLEY

Wicherley earnes hard for what he gaines;
Hee wants no judgment, and hee spares noe paines;
Hee oftentimes excells, and att the best
Committs lesse faults than any of the rest.

17th C   *John Wilmot, Earl of Rochester*

The playwright William Wycherley was born at Clive near Shrewsbury in 1604 and spent much of his adult life at Clive Hall.

A SHROPSHIRE LAD
*(Captain Webb, the first man to swim the English Channel, was a
relation by marriage of Mary Webb)*

The gas was on in the Institute,
  The flare was up in the gym,
A man was running a mineral line,
  A lass was singing a hymn,
When Captain Webb the Dawley man,
  Captain Webb from Dawley,
Came swimming along in the old canal
  That carried the bricks to Lawley,
      Swimming along –
      Swimming along –
      Swimming along from the Severn,
And paying a call at Dawley Bank while swimming along to Heaven.

The sun shone low on the railway line
  And over the bricks and stacks,
And in at the upstairs windows
  Of the Dawley houses' backs,
When we saw the ghost of Captain Webb,
  Webb in a water sheeting,
Come dripping along in a bathing dress
  To the Saturday evening meeting.
      Dripping along –
      Dripping along –
      To the Congregational Hall;
Dripping and still he rose over the sill and faded away in a wall.

There wasn't a man in Oakengates
  That hadn't got hold of the tale,
And over the valley in Ironbridge,
  And round by Coalbrookdale,
How Captain Webb the Dawley man,
  Captain Webb from Dawley,
Rose rigid and dead from the old canal
  That carries the bricks to Lawley.
      Rigid and dead –
      Rigid and dead –
      To the Saturday congregation,
Paying a call at Dawley Bank on his way to his destination.

1940   *John Betjeman*

NEW TOWN
(Telford)

Strewn among ancient hills
larks still spiralling
where raddled earth
has thrown its slagheaps
refuse of small scattered communities
loose on the sick surface
creates a textured soil.
Machines and excavators
impacting over old mines
shovel rough gravel
level and smooth
fill hollows in a half-green landscape.

Here
where Oakengates, Wellington, Shifnal
all proclaim people
signify vital places
the new town slowly grows.
Between one journey and the next
blue diesel nosing its way
through wreckage of a past revolution
you see its certain stride
towards identity. At this early hour
sun rising on sour fields
a trickle of children, satchels slung
emerge from bright boxes
run over waste land
sing a new day's song.

1972   *M.A.B. Jones*

THE LADY OF TONG

Painted Lady, lightly borne on ancient breezes, down to Tong,
Its forest quick with rooting hogs, its lake with silver turning shoals
Below the rearing castle walls of Leofric's descendants.

Gilded Mary, Holy Lady, light and shade of chapel windows,
At her feet a gift of roses, rested each midsummer's day
By serfs to bless their great providers, mighty lords of Tong.

Isabella, lady founder, proud before the altar rail,
Her masses said, her church completed, destined now for Benedicta,
Stanleys, Vernons, yet to shine in Haddon Hall and Tong.

Alabaster lady sleeping, cool beside the altar rail,
Her castle gone, she lies unheeding, pale beneath the tourists' gaze,
A broken fawn against her feet and roses in her hand.

1994   *Heather Wilson*

TONG CHURCH

A hushed and faded sense of damp decay
Pervades this ancient church, where
The dusty weight
Of time hangs heavy in the vaulted air.
Here, age-black pews are peopled by the ghosts
Of knights and villagers, whose long-dead prayers
Drown out our whispers. Cold and remote
White marble effigies lie in pairs.
Tier upon tier, stone linen, headress, sword and shield,
Locked in perpetual piety they wait –
Self-certain of their resurrection.
The power they once held has faded and they yield
To dust and history. No rustic genuflection
Now pays tribute to those generations gone,
Yet they can still remind us of our own mortality.
A different image on one tomb is etched in bronze.
Black with a thousand rubbings, it reveals today's reality
For common men get down before him on their knees
Only when they have paid the vicar rubbing fees,
And thus the graven image of their search
Continues to maintain the fabric of the church.

1987   *Allister Fraser*

THE GHOST OF MR HERBERT DAWSON
Choirmaster and organist of All Saints, Baschurch. Died 1920

He has slipped in between the familiar stones,
mossed himself into the mortar.
This is his niche, and here
he has inscribed his voice
– note by frail latin note –
in glassy chants, only half audible
under the empty shivers of silence.
This was his life's dwelling place, now
he will not let go.

He is an odd indelible phrase
on the palimpsest of this dark church militant,
an etheric chime mewed in the cinnabar stones
that press the architecture into the earth,
each red, edged stone hewn with the precision
of a perfect sword-cut. Intransigent geometry,
echoing the pulpit-thundered lessons
of prohibition, stricture, obedience.
There is no God but my God.

Herbert Dawson, O Man Greatly Beloved:
his music clarioned glory into matins,
harmonies of harp and lamb lifted spirits.
His psalm now is a print of cold air,
faint descant flickering under the altar shadows
where plainsong of scriptures, layer
on dusty layer, shore up the walls
against whatever the threat
of the next incoming tide.
Once, it was always the bitter Welsh, their fires
rosing the church's sober aqueous light.
Now, Cadwalader's rushing engines roar enough
to shake loose the restless graves
so they sway like jostling ice;
slanted white crosses, flags of protest
cut out of marble, obsidian
the crowds of history rising...

And in the long awaited hour of the last battle
the day of revelation, dissolution?
Amongst the patient ghosts and quiet spirits
goes Herbert Dawson ascending,
fluent notes waterfalling out
studding the air with joyous brilliance
as at last he celebrates the long bright freedom
promised to his soul.

1994   *Rose Flint*

from
HAWKSTONE PARK

By this stupendous place we pass
  Thro' walks extended wide,
Pressing the banks of tender grass
  Along the mountain's side.
Thro' avenues of cheerful green,
  Where richest meadows smile,
Where gentle flocks of playful mien
  Their harmless hours beguile....

Ye secret springs, ye gentle rills,
  That fill the humble vale,
That murmuring rise among the hills,
  And wash the lowly dale....

Thro' rocks of solid stone we're led,
  Thro' hills of various form,
Thro' openings, cliffs, which rear their head
  Against the coming storm....

Viewing the rocky-mantled dome
  In secret shades retir'd:
Here beams of light thro' colour'd glass
  Bring to our raptur's view
The Grotto's treasures, as we pass,
  In all their brilliant hue.
Here various shells from every shore,
  And plac'd with nicest skill;
Here fossils too delight the eye
  In this enchanting place,
And with the sea-shells seem to vie
  In beauty and in grace.

18th C   *John Salmon*

THE NORTON-IN-HALES WAKE

Last March, it being a holiday time,
When I was young and just in my prime,
To Norton Wake it was my intent,
I dressed myself up, and away I went.

There was Roger the plough man,
Sally and Ally, and Nan;
We each took a lass, we tripped it along,
And, when we got there, there was a great throng.

There was some crying Banburys and some crying cakes;
My lads and my lasses, let's keep up the Wakes!
Some crying Banburys as big as the egg of a pout,
And gingerbread junks as big as my foot.

We eat and we ate, and we ate and we eat,
Till we could not eat more, they were so good and sweet;
So Bob treated Ally and Ralph treated Sally,
And I bought a fig cake for my Mally.

Then next was a bull that they brought to the stake,
And this was all done some fun for to make.
He gave them a toss and a terrible throw,
Threw the dogs in the air, and the folks tumbled o'er,
Such pulling and hauling and shouting and bawling
As I never saw in my life before.

19th C   *Trad*

LARGE HEATH AT WHIXALL MOSS

Here, the flat expanses
(not entirely featureless as fabled
nor as boggy after two dry summers)
where distant Curlews cry
and Meadow Pipits parachute
where Dragonflies dart and dazzle
and insects buzz and bite
where Heather's pink bejewels peat
and Cottongrass shivers by dark pools,
it bobs and flutters tantalizingly close
and never seems to settle long
– except when skies turn overcast –
or near enough to photograph.

And one paltry print,
its row of eyespots visible
against the background grey and brown,
low down through blurring grasses,
must suffice for all this;
can only hold a fragment
of this precious beautiful-bleak scene.

1994   *Brian Mitchell*

THE WOMEN OF WEM

The women of Wem and a few musketeers
Beat the Lord Capel and all his cavaliers.

17th C   *Trad*

An incident in the Civil War when some of the women saved the town by dressing in red
cloaks and deceiving the attacking Royalists as to the strength of the defending garrison.

THE RUINS OF WHITTINGTON CASTLE

Oh, Whittington, amongst thy tow'rs,
  Pleased did my early childhood stray,
Bask'd on thy walls in sunny hours,
And pull'd thy moss, and pluck'd thy flowers,
  Fully many a truant day.
And midst the weed-bewilder'd ways
I've thought on Giants, Hags and Fays,
Or aught that in those elfish days
  My eager eye hath read;
And hying home at evening tide,
Scared if the circling bat I spied,
I've pass'd in haste thy portals wide
  With no unpleasing dread.

And oft I've stood in mute amaze,
With fearful inquest fond to gaze,
  When labourers 'mid the stones
Deep in the mortar-mingled ground
Huge gyves and iron fetters found,
  And canker crusted bones.

Though oft were found, of antique mold,
Quaint bottles, burnished as with gold:
  Branch'd antlers of the deer:
And fragments toss'd that bowls had been;
With relics more, yet shewn, I ween,
  Within the mansion here.

And much I've mused with strange delight
On him, the faintly-figured knight,
On fiery steed, Fitz-Gwarine hight
Be-rhymed with rustic verse...
In ancient days of high renown,
Not always did yon castle frown
With ivy-crested brow;
Nor were its walls with moss embrown'd,
Nor hung the lanky weeds around
  That fringe its ruins now.

Other hangings deck'd the wall,
Where now the nodding foxgloves tall
  Their spotty hoods unfold;
Harebells there with bugloss vie,
And gilliflowers of yellow dye,
Seem now, to musing Fancy's eye,
To mock the mimic tapestry
  That flaunted there of old.

Other guests than yon lone bird,
And other music here was heard,
    In times of better days;
Festive revelry went round,
The board with blushing goblets crown'd,
And costly carpets clad the ground
    Where now yon cattle graze.

Days were those of splendour high,
Days of hospitality,
    When to his rich domain
Welcom'd many a crested knight,
Welcom'd many a lady bright,
    Fitz-Gwarine of Lorraine.

19th C   *John F.M. Dovaston*

PLACE RHYMES

The finest pastime that is under the sun
Is Whipping the Cat at Albrighton!

19th C.   *Anon*

As sure as Hodnet sends the wind,
A rainy day will Drayton find.

Trad

It rains, it hails, it batters, it blows,
The Tibberton girls are washing their clothes.

Trad

ELLESMERE

This rhyme laments the down-grading of the famous "Wonder" coach that originally ran
from Shrewsbury to London driven by the legendary Samuel Hayward of Ellesmere.

Adown the Wyle Cop, prince of coachmen, no more
Shall you ever be seen touching up your swift four,
But spare us, O Hayward, O spare us, forbear,
From driving the "Wonder" with only a pair.

19th C   *Anon*

PLACE RHYMES

A new church, an old steeple,
A drunken parson, and a wicked people.
Amen,
Says the clerk of Wem.

Trad

Ellesmere, Oswestry, Whitchurch and Wem,
In four letters spell me them.

Trad

from
**THE VERY OLD MAN:
or The Life of Thomas Parr***

Good wholsome labour was his exercise,
Down with the Lamb, & with the Lark would rise,
In myre and toyling sweat he spent the day,
And (to his Teame) he whistled Time away:
The Cock his night-Clock, and till day was done,
His Watch, and chief Sun-Diall, was the Sun.
He was of old Pithagoras opinion,
The green cheese was most wholsome with an onion,
Coarse Mesclin bread, and for his daily swig,
Milk, Butter-milk, and Water, Whey, and Whig;
Sometimes Metheglin, and by fortune happy,
He sometimes sip't a Cup of Ale most nappy,
Cyder, or Perry, when he did repair
T'a Whitson Ale, Wake, Wedding, or a Fair,
Or when in Christmas time he was a Guest
At his good Land-lords house amongst the rest:
Else he had little leasure Time to waste,
Or (at the Alehouse) huffe-cap Ale to taste.
Nor did he ever hunt a Taverne Fox,
Nere knew a Coach, Tobacco, or the Pox;
His Physick was good Butter, which the soyle
Of Salop yields, more sweet than Candy oyle,
And Garlick he esteem'd above the rate
Of Venice-Triacle, or best Mithridate.
He entertain'd no Gowt, no Ache he felt,
The ayre was good, and temp'rat where he dwelt,
Whilst Mavisses, and sweet tongu'd Nightingales
Did chant him Roundelayes, and Madrigals.
Thus living within bounds of Natures Lawes,
Of his long lasting life may be some cause.

1635   *John Taylor*

---

*Parr came from Winnington in Shropshire, and was apparently blessed with incredible longevity, reputedly living through the reigns of ten sovereigns! He is buried in Westminster Abbey.

THE OLD MILKING PARLOUR
(Ruyton XI Towns)

Brick on brick
this so, so solid
edifice stands its ground
four-square, plain.
Yet in spring a lilac,
washed white, foams
against one wall

with all transformed

temporarily: inside too
the hopeful lick of paint
a table, chair, books
and papers; solitude.
Only the fox-shadowed
rabbit-startled
view – through open
window – to distract
me from this page.

Across the yard

the house. There
the chores; the day-to-day.
Here the space
for fantasy, the dreams
of beasts that came
at dusk. Clumbered
shapes, with eyes of night,
and breath of clover
from the greening grass.

So often, now

byres and barns convert
to the need of change;
but here the old milking
parlour is held in trust
for a far dream of evening
when, perhaps,
cattle will come again.

1991   *Brenda Whincup*

(Awarded first prize, Wrekin Writers' Open Poetry Competition, 1991)

from
IN PRAISE OF OSWESTRY

Hill-countryman in younger days,
Now with grey hairs I've changed my ways;
My faltering steps prefer the town,
Within its walls I'll settle down.
My jaded stomach milk would scorn,
And calls for physic night and morn.
A wandering poet near life's goal
Prefers his flask and pewter bowl,
Warmth and comfort and friendly cheer,
Fresh meat, white flour, and good beer.
The timbered homes of lowland lea
Restore my health like the green tree,
Hence the home which shall be mine
In Marchland where are mead and wine;
Generous and true, a friendly town,
Gracious, gifted, of high renown;
The castle with its curtain wall
Famed far as Rome above them all:
Oswald's town, where Christ is loved,
To the Conqueror a treasure proved.

The London of our Owain's land,
With orchards rich and wine-shops grand,
A school that's free, and of wide fame,
The town of preachers of good name;
In a temple rich the Host they raise –
Men in grammar and metrics beyond all praise,
A church supreme, and jewelled chalice,
Clear bells, and an organ in God's palace,
A tuneful choir – a well-trained band,
Vestments famed throughout the land;
Where find you clergy as good and bright
As they who serve in that temple white?
In coiffure and dress no women excel
Those who in Oswald's city dwell.
Adorned in Cheapside's merchandise,
Harmonious her citizens, and wise.

15th C   *Gul Guto'r (trans. D.M. Lloyd)*

INDEX OF POETS